INTRODUCTION

There are tales of King Arthur all over Europe, many claiming to be actual histories. These stories have been described as "not all a lie, nor all true, nor all fable, nor all known". It may be that there lies some truth behind all the stories and the name "Arthur" given to any local or national hero.

In Britain it is generally thought that a Christian leader, and Arthur figure, lived in the 5th century and fought against the invading pagan Saxons. The Arthur legends are therefore concentrated in the Celtic areas of Britain, in Scotland, Wales and the West Country.

The continuing popularity of Arthurian tales indicate what a powerful hold they have on the public imagination. We hope this little book stimulates your imagination further.

Whilst compiling this book we have on occasions come across spelling variations.

To those King Arthur enthusiasts who may pick up on these variations we ask for forgiveness if you insist we are incorrect.   L.C.

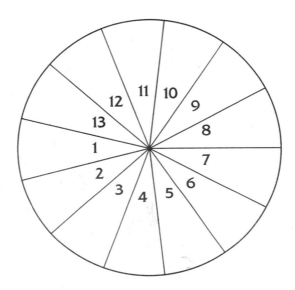

At King Arthur's Hall in Tintagel there is a copy of the Round Table which gives the seating arrangements. From the clues given below can you discover who sat where?

1. Arthur was seated at number 4 with Percival and Lancelot next to him.

2. Kay was at number 10 with Gawain, then Gaheris to his left.

3. Galahad sat between Percival and Bors, with Gareth next-but-one on his left.

4. Bedivere had Tristan and Gaheris as his neighbours, while Geraint had Lamorak and Gareth as his.

How many words can you make from CAMELOT? We managed 36. Can you do better?

All words must have at least 4 letters. No plurals or proper names.

2   RIDDLE

My first is in sword and also in shield,
My second's in winner but not in yield.
My third you will find in magic and trance,
My fourth is in dagger but not in lance.
My fifth you will find in horse but not steed,
My sixth is in done but not in deed.
My whole is what the knights went to kill,
Living alone in a cave on the hill.

What am I?

Can you find these characters in the grid opposite?

Arthur	Nabur
Bedivere	Oberon
Camal	Percival
Drudwas	Quintelian
Elaine	Rowland
Finbeus	Sigfried
Gawain	Tristan
Hoel	Uther
Isolda	Vortigern
Joseph	Wigolais
Kay	eXcalibur
Lancelot	Yglais
Mordred	Zelotes

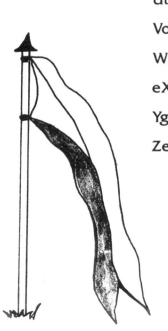

Q	D	E	R	D	R	O	M	F	A	B	M	E	R
N	U	A	D	L	O	S	I	O	E	O	U	N	O
I	S	I	N	A	R	M	B	D	S	E	E	I	W
A	S	A	N	E	I	E	I	U	X	N	N	A	L
W	T	R	H	T	R	V	E	C	H	R	E	L	A
A	A	T	R	O	E	B	A	T	E	H	U	E	N
G	U	H	N	R	N	L	W	G	R	I	L	L	D
D	A	U	E	I	I	I	I	S	N	N	A	A	E
R	Y	R	F	B	G	T	E	A	J	L	N	V	I
U	G	E	U	O	R	T	T	O	N	C	C	I	R
D	L	R	L	O	O	S	S	A	G	A	E	C	F
W	A	A	V	L	I	E	B	K	E	M	L	R	G
A	I	N	E	R	P	U	A	D	S	A	O	E	I
S	S	Z	T	H	R	Y	H	O	E	L	T	P	S

The letters left over will tell you what these characters have in common.

In the past they were very fond of naming their belongings, particularly their articles of war. Below is a list of some of the belongings of King Arthur, with their names. Can you fit their names into the grid opposite.

SWORDS

Chastiefol

Excalibur

Honoree

Marmyadose

Sequence

OTHERS

Cabal (dog)

Carnwennan (dagger)

Clydno (see opposite)

Courechouse (horse)

Dagonet (fool)

Goswhit (helmet)

Gwen (Mantle of Invisibility)

Prydwen (ship)

Ron (lance)

Spumador (horse)

Wygar (hauberk)

The letters in circles will reveal what article Clydno was.

5

LOGIC PROBLEM
RESCUING DAMSELS IN DISTRESS

1   The battleaxe was used to kill the boar and it was the serpent that held Isolda captive.

2   Lancelot fought the dragon but not to rescue Gwyneth.

3   The lancer who freed Melora was not Galahad or Lancelot.

4   Elaine was saved by Sir Kay who did not have a battleaxe or fight the wizard.

5   Gawain was an archer and did not save Anna, for she was rescued by a swordsman.

Using the clues given above, can you work out which Knight rescued which damsel from which enemy and what weapon he used to do so.

	ELAINE	ISOLDA	ANNA	MELORA	GWYNETH	DRAGON	GIANT	BOAR	WIZARD	SERPENT	LANCE	SWORD	BATTLEAXE	DAGGER	BOW
GAWAIN															
LANCELOT															
GALAHAD															
MORDRED															
KAY															
LANCE															
SWORD															
BATTLEAXE															
DAGGER															
BOW															
DRAGON															
GIANT															
BOAR															
WIZARD															
SERPENT															

NAME	ENEMY	DAMSEL	WEAPON
GAWAIN			
LANCELOT			
GALAHAD			
MORDRED			
KAY			

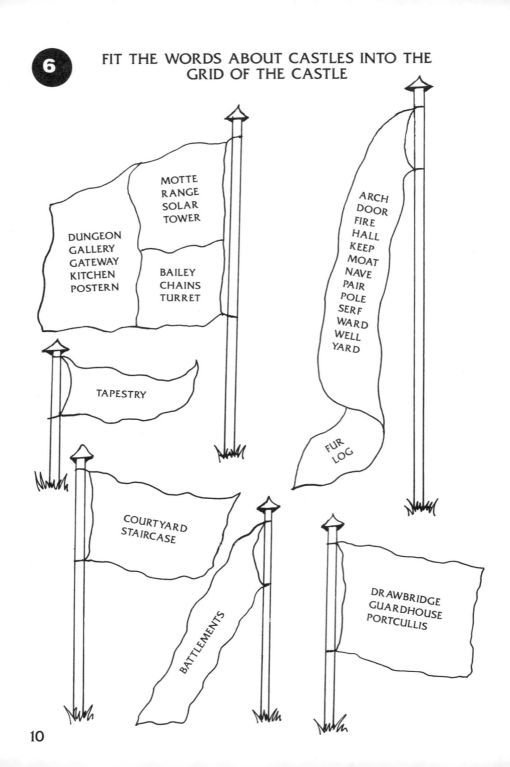

FIT THE WORDS ABOUT CASTLES INTO THE GRID OF THE CASTLE

MOTTE
RANGE
SOLAR
TOWER

DUNGEON
GALLERY
GATEWAY
KITCHEN
POSTERN

BAILEY
CHAINS
TURRET

ARCH
DOOR
FIRE
HALL
KEEP
MOAT
NAVE
PAIR
POLE
SERF
WARD
WELL
YARD

TAPESTRY

FUR
LOG

COURTYARD
STAIRCASE

BATTLEMENTS

DRAWBRIDGE
GUARDHOUSE
PORTCULLIS

The letters in circles will spell the name of a famous
castle in Arthurian legend.

SUPERNATURAL BEINGS

The Tales of King Arthur contain many supernatural beings, ranging from gods to wizards, animals and giants. Some are listed here, taken from tales from all over Europe. Can you find them in the grid opposite?

Aillean	Guinebaut
Alcina	Gwyneth
Anu	Hellekin
Beli	Klingsor
Blaise	Lug
Caelia	Mabon
Camille	Mabuz
Ceridwen	Maeve
Coel	Magog
Diane	Marsique
Don	Mazadan
Eliavres	Menw
Elergia	Merlin
Eriu	Oberon
Esclarimonde	Owyn
Evrain	Rathlean
Florisdelfa	Tanaburs
Gog	

A	N	I	C	L	A	I	G	R	E	L	E
O	B	E	R	O	N	T	E	H	C	S	F
E	G	D	S	I	N	L	A	E	I	L	U
N	O	U	A	R	L	N	R	A	O	G	I
N	I	R	I	I	U	I	L	R	I	O	R
A	V	K	M	N	D	B	I	U	N	G	E
E	E	A	E	W	E	S	A	H	G	D	L
L	C	A	E	L	D	B	R	N	N	G	I
L	B	N	R	E	L	A	A	O	A	H	A
I	S	E	L	O	T	E	M	U	O	T	V
A	F	F	L	H	S	I	H	N	T	E	R
G	A	E	L	I	R	G	A	L	G	N	E
O	O	E	M	A	D	D	N	O	U	Y	S
C	A	E	L	I	A	Z	G	I	C	W	E
N	N	C	A	Z	U	A	E	S	L	G	V
W	S	N	A	B	M	A	B	O	N	K	E
E	E	M	A	R	S	I	Q	U	E	T	A
E	R	M	E	R	L	I	N	Y	W	O	M

The unused letters will spell a collection
of other supernatural beings
from the Arthurian Tales

QUIZ

1   Who is regarded as the father of King Arthur?

2   With whom was Guinevere unfaithful to Arthur?

3   Who fought the Green Knight?

4   What does Avalon mean?

5   Who gave King Arthur the sword of Excalibur?

6   Who was the uncle of Tristan and Iseult?

7   Who planted the Glastonbury Thorn?

8   Where in Cornwall was Arthur conceived?

9   Which monument is Merlin alleged to have built?

10   Who is the ruler of the Wasteland in the Grail Legends?

11   Which country was called "Merlin's Precinct"?

12   What breed of bird did Arthur have as a pet?

13   Where, in 1191AD, was the alleged grave of Arthur found?

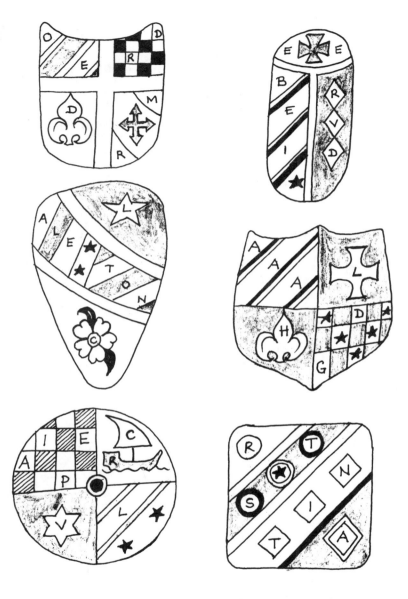

Find out who these shields belong to by
unjumbling the letters on them

PIECES OF ARMOUR

Fit these names of parts of armour into the grid opposite.

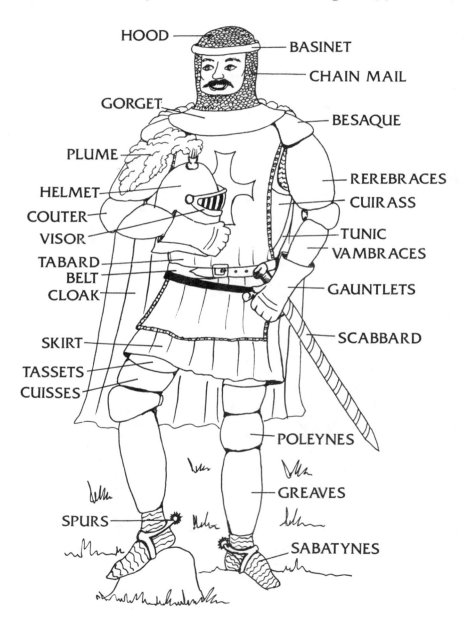

HOOD

BASINET

CHAIN MAIL

GORGET

BESAQUE

PLUME

REREBRACES

HELMET

CUIRASS

COUTER

TUNIC

VISOR

VAMBRACES

TABARD

BELT

CLOAK

GAUNTLETS

SKIRT

SCABBARD

TASSETS

CUISSES

POLEYNES

GREAVES

SPURS

SABATYNES

The letters in circles will spell the name
of a famous order of chivalry.

Passes through Maze

Pulls Sword from Stone

Red Knight

Tames Wild Hawk

Wins Jousting Tournament

Uses Merlin Spell

Meet Herm.

Sir Galahad was the son of Sir Lancelot and went in search of the Holy Grail. Can you work out what route he took to the Grail by going from one adventure to the next. You should experience all the adventures and not cross your own path.

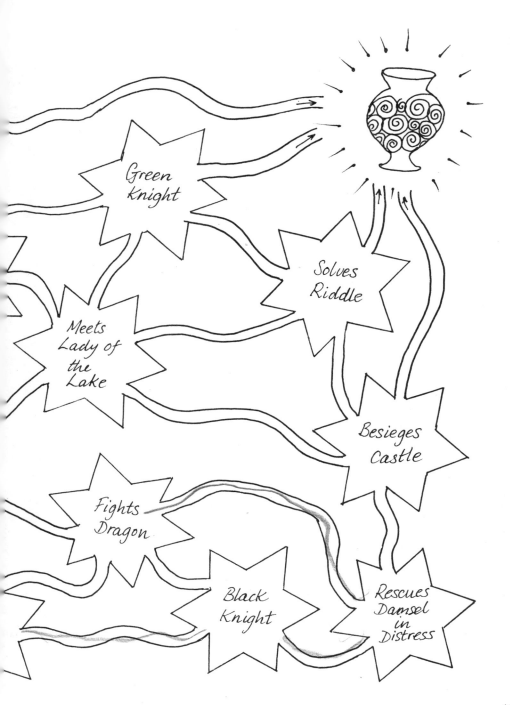

Green Knight

Solves Riddle

Meets Lady of the Lake

Besieges Castle

Fights Dragon

Black Knight

Rescues Damsel in Distress

M	T	H	T	S	C	H	E	S	T	E	R
A	E	Y	R	U	B	D	A	C	N	B	E
R	G	R	I	S	M	B	A	N	T	A	T
T	U	U	B	S	T	O	A	O	N	D	S
E	I	B	U	A	T	L	L	L	A	O	E
H	N	N	I	B	M	E	E	D	N	N	H
G	N	O	T	A	M	D	O	R	E	O	C
R	I	T	C	A	R	B	O	N	E	K	N
U	O	S	C	G	G	U	F	O	R	E	I
B	N	A	C	N	G	E	D	C	G	L	W
N	F	L	K	E	Y	O	L	A	S	L	A
I	W	G	M	D	L	B	N	L	A	I	L
D	N	O	M	H	C	I	R	E	N	W	C
E	N	A	R	I	E	D	D	D	I	I	L
T	A	A	D	L	A	S	R	O	D	C	U
D	O	U	G	L	A	S	O	N	N	N	D

The remaining unused letters will spell out
where King Arthur was killed.

CASTLES AND BATTLEGROUNDS

Dinas
Orsa
Camelot
Tintagel
Richmond
Carbonek
Key
Rougemont
Winchester
Marte
Cadbury
Glastonbury
Edinburgh
Dore
Agned
Lacon

Alclud
Annwfn
Glein
Douglas
Bassus
Celidon
Deira
Mold
Chester
Tribuit
Badon
Camlann
Caledon
Greenan
Dol
Guinnion
Kelliwic

These castles and battles (and many sites) are recorded in Arthurian legends from all over Europe. Can you find the ones above in the grid opposite.

	EIDDILIG	LLYWARCH	NASIENS	MORFRAN	SANDEF	VALLEY	MOUNTAIN	MARSH	ISLAND	FOREST	POTION	RING	WAND	HORN	STONE	SWAN	BOAR	RAVEN	HOUND	STAG
DAMART																				
MERLIN																				
MORGAN LE FAY																				
GWION																				
WITIGE																				
SWAN																				
BOAR																				
RAVEN																				
HOUND																				
STAG																				
POTION																				
RING																				
WAND																				
HORN																				
STONE																				
VALLEY																				
MOUNTAIN																				
MARSH																				
ISLAND																				
FOREST																				

MAGICIAN	ON	INTO	HOW	WHERE
DAMART				
MERLIN				
MORGAN LE FAY				
GWION				
WITIGE				

WORKING MAGIC LOGIC PROBLEM

Using the clues given below, can you work out which magician used which magic tool to change which person into something strange and where they lived.

1. It was a magician with an initial 'M' who changed his opponent into a raven.

2. The magician from the mountain used a potion to create a swan. It was not Damart, because he changed Morfran to a stag.

3. Eiddilig was turned into a raven, but not in the valley, because a magic horn was used.

4. Morgan did not change Nasiens and did not use a wand, unlike Gwion, or a stone.

5. Llywarch lived in the forest and Sandef came from an island, where a ring was to be found.

6. Witige changed his foe into a hound.

7. The marsh dweller was not changed by a wand or stone.

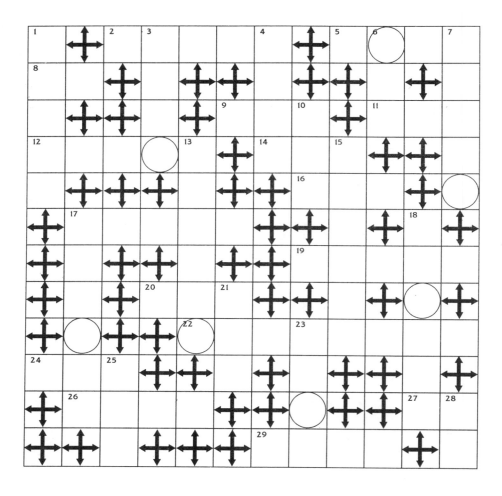

The letters in circles provide the name of the place
where Tristan fought the dragon.

TRISTAN AND THE DRAGON

One day Tristan set off to ---- (5 across) the ------ (13 down) who
had destroyed much of the country. he found the creature's ----
(3 down) and called out a challenge. Out of --- (11 across) cave
crawled the beast, with smoke and fire coming from its --------
(22 across). Tristan's ----- (1 down) reared in ------ (15 down),
throwing Tristan to the ground, then turned and ---- (29 across).
--- (10 down) the knight was -- (8 across) his --- (9 across), but
he would not ----- (7 down) and held his ------- (17 down) in front
of him to keep the --- (20 across) breath off his body. The awful
creature was over five metres long from the --- (21 down) of his
head to the tip -- (28 down) his ---- (23 down). Tristan threw his
----- (17 across) and hit the creature in the throat, piercing the
------ (18 down) which covered his body. Warm, putrid ----- (2
across) gushed from the wound, making the ground --- (16
across) and slippery. Tristan slipped and fell ---- (4 down) and
the dragon's claws caught his --- (25 down) twisting his knee and
making him feel --- (24 across), but he would --- (14 across) give
in. Tristan had to ----- (19 across) the monster to make it --- (6
down) go, -- (27 across) he pretended to be ---- (26 across). The
dragon set him free for a moment, so Tristan quickly grabbed his
----- (12 across) and cut off the dragon's head in one great swipe.
Arthur was so grateful he made Tristan a Knight of the Round
Table.

THE THIRTEEN TREASURES OF BRITAIN

These articles were obtained by one means or another from their owners by a magician who kept them in his house of glass. Can you fit them into the grid. The circled letters will then reveal the magician's name.

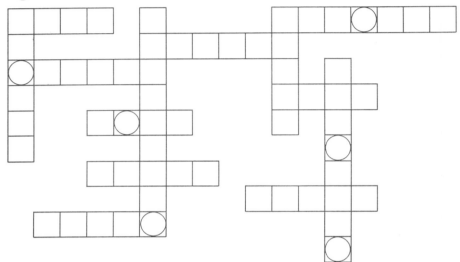

Dyrnwyn, the SWORD of Rhydderch Hall.

The HAMPER of Gwyddno Garanhir.

The HORN of Bran Galad.

The CHARIOT of Morgan.

The HALTER of Clydno Eiddyn.

The KNIFE of Lanfrodedd.

The CAULDRON of Diwrnach the Giant.

The WHETSTONE of Tudwal Tudglyd.

The COAT of Padarn Redcoat.

The CROCK of Rhygenydd.

The DISH of Rhygenydd.

The *Gwyddbwll BOARD of Gwenddolan.

Arthur's MANTLE of Invisibility.

* A game similar to chess.

My first is in damsel but not in distress.
My second's in errand but not in quest.
My third is in legend but not in tale,
My fourth is in chalice but not in grail.
My fifth is in castle but not in court,
My sixth is in battle that has to be fought.
My seventh's in glory and also in bold,
My last is in Knight whose story is told.

Who am I?

How many words can you make from the grid below? The letter 'C' must be in every word.

R	U	E
A	C	I
X	B	L

They must have 4 letters at least, no proper names or plurals. We have managed to get 21.

B	N	E	D	D	A	D	A	P	S	Y	T
H	L	V	T	W	A	D	D	E	L	L	W
C	N	A	L	A	B	A	C	C	U	C	R
A	I	D	N	T	H	E	A	E	N	M	C
N	C	E	A	C	N	T	I	A	G	R	H
R	O	A	I	A	H	R	F	C	A	A	T
W	R	M	G	P	C	A	N	D	G	O	R
A	F	R	A	T	R	O	R	R	O	B	W
L	U	L	I	I	B	U	I	D	R	R	Y
B	U	T	T	A	I	N	B	T	R	E	T
G	E	H	N	D	G	E	R	N	I	D	H
P	O	L	A	A	L	O	E	I	B	N	T
C	A	N	L	A	G	W	C	O	E	U	O
A	K	E	G	E	N	R	H	R	S	L	L
R	T	O	S	E	O	R	A	T	S	B	E
L	G	E	H	L	L	U	A	G	O	R	M

The unused letters will spell the name
of another creature

GIANTS, DWARFS, MONSTERS AND BEASTS
IN THE TALES OF ARTHUR

AFANC

BELAGOG

BLANCHARD

BLUNDERBOAR

CABAL

CARL

CATH PALUG

DRUIDAN

EVADEAM

FROCIN

GARGANTUA

GRINGALET

HENWEN

LLUAGOR

MELOT

NABON

ORRIBES

PETITCRIEU

RITHO

ROGES

TROINT

TWADDELL

TWRCH TRWYTH

URGAN

WRNACH

YSPADADDEN

Above are the names of some of the strange creatures mentioned in the Arthurian myths. Can you find them in the grid opposite?

In Tintagel there are the coats of arms and names of the Knights who formed the Fellowship of Knights.

Palomides	Gawain
Persides	Griflet
Constantine	Geraint
Galahad	Lancelot
Pertelope	Percivale
Bellangere	Tristran
Balin	Bors
Lucas	Ector
Priamus	Ban
Ironside	Kay
Lamorak	Owen
Pellias	Gareth
Gaheris	Pelles
Dragonet	Lionel
Bedivere	Mordred
Breunot	

B	E	K	I	E	L	A	V	I	C	R	E	P
E	E	N	N	T	O	N	U	E	R	B	G	A
D	R	L	I	T	R	I	S	T	R	A	N	L
I	O	D	L	T	G	A	L	A	H	A	D	O
V	T	E	A	A	N	W	N	I	L	A	B	M
E	C	R	R	T	N	A	K	A	Y	D	H	I
R	E	D	P	A	T	G	T	U	R	R	S	D
E	G	R	B	R	N	N	E	S	G	A	L	E
I	R	O	N	S	I	D	E	R	N	G	A	S
G	I	M	K	G	A	A	R	W	E	O	N	E
A	F	L	A	A	R	I	M	E	O	N	C	D
H	L	I	R	R	E	A	L	U	T	E	E	I
E	E	O	O	E	G	H	A	L	S	T	L	S
R	T	N	M	T	B	O	R	S	E	L	O	R
I	L	E	A	H	L	U	C	A	S	P	T	E
S	E	L	L	E	P	O	L	E	T	R	E	P

The letters left over will spell out the building where the chivalrous artifacts may be found.

THE CHILDREN OF KING ARTHUR
(Allegedly)

Adelut

Amr

Arthur (see below)

Borre

Ellen

Gwydre

Gyneth

Ilinot

Llacheu

Loholt

Melora

Mordred

Morgan (The Black)

Patrick (The Red)

Rowland

Tom (The Red Rose Knight)

The letters in circles spell out the nick-name of Arthur, son of King Arthur.

RIDDLE

My first is in joust and also in fight
My second in strong but not in might
My third is in damsel not in distress
My fourth is in rode but not in dress.
My fifth is in player and also in fool
My sixth is in river but not in pool
My seventh in knight but not in court
My eighth is in castle but not in fort
My ninth is in float and also in drown
My tenth is in black but not in brown
My last is in found and also in won
The whole together is Arthur's son.

Fill in the letters of this Crossword about Knights in Armour using the grid below and the clue opposite.

19				15	6	5	7	17	2		23	20	10	9	7	13
9		18		5				9						10		
2	20	24	10	6	9	11	13	6	2		25	10	9	7	20	6
2		13		7		9		25		9		10		24		
1		26		9	7	13		9	10	11		11		6		
13	8	2	20	1		5		1		26	22	20	10	25	26	
		5			3	9	26	2	1	13		24		14		
23	20	20	1	26		25		10		1	20	10	25	1	4	
20		6		7		12		24				5				
10			17	20	10	26	13		5		3	9	24	26	13	26
13		10		9		6		26		3		2				
26	22	9	6		5		2		11	4	26	2	13	10	4	
2		12		9	1	20	24	25			5		13			
	13		1		10			21	20	24	26	2	26			
11	9	6	2	1	13		13	10	9		6		26			

A	B	C	D	E	F	G	H	I	J	K	L	M

N	O	P	Q	R	S	T	U	V	W	X	Y	Z

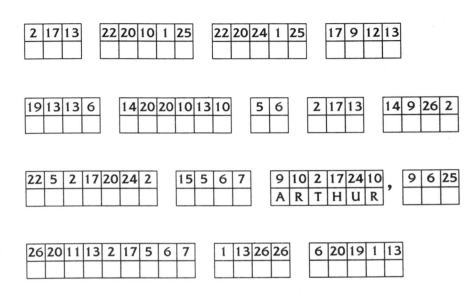

2	17	13

22	20	10	1	25

22	20	24	1	25

17	9	12	13

19	13	13	6

14	20	20	10	13	10

5	6

2	17	13

14	9	26	2

22	5	2	17	20	24	2

15	5	6	7

9	10	2	17	24	10
A	R	T	H	U	R

,

9	6	25

26	20	11	13	2	17	5	6	7

1	13	26	26

6	20	19	1	13

2	20	25	9	4

20	10

5	6

2	17	13

23	24	2	24	10	13

Extract from "King Arthur's Great Hall of Chivalry" by The Sword in the Stone Ltd.

ANSWERS

1 1 Bors, 2 Galahad, 3 Percival,
   4 Arthur, 5 Lancelot, 6 Tristan,
   7 Bedivere, 8 Gaheris, 9 Gawain,
   10 Kay, 11 Lamorak, 12 Geraint,
   13 Gareth

2 Dragon

3 Famous names in the Arthurian
   Legends

4 Cauldron

5

NAME	ENEMY	DAMSEL	WEAPON
Gawain	Serpent	Isolda	Bow
Lancelot	Dragon	Anna	Sword
Galahad	Boar	Gwynwth	Battleaxe
Mordred	Wizard	Melora	Lance
Kay	Giant	Elaine	Dagger

6 Perilous

7 The Nine Hags of Gloucester

8 1 Uther Pendragon, 2 Lancelot,
   3 Gawain, 4 Isle of Apples, 5 The
   Lady of the Lake, 6 King Mark of
   Cornwall, 7 Joseph of Arimathea,
   8 Tintagel, 9 Stonehenge, 10 The
   Fisher King (Anfortas), 11 Britain,
   12 A Parrot, 13 Glastonbury

9 1 Mordred, 2 Bedivere, 3 Lancelot, 4
   Galahad, 5 Percival, 6 Tristan

10 Knights Templar

11 The Battle of Badon

12

MAGICIAN	ON	INTO	HOW	WHERE
Damart	Morfran	Stag	Stone	Valley
Merlin	Nasiens	Swan	Potion	Mountain
Morgan Le Fay	Eiddilig	Raven	Horn	Marsh
Gwion	Llywarch	Boar	Wand	Forest
Witige	Sandef	Hound	Ring	Island

13 Ireland

14 Merlin

15 Lancelot

16 The Magical Black Horse

17 King Arthur's Great Hall

18 "The Little"

19 Tom O'Lincoln

20 "The world would have been poorer
    in the past without King Arthur, and
    something less noble today or in the
    future."